This book belongs to

English - Norwegian

duck   Date _____

and

duck and

duck
duck
duck
duck
duck

Make a sentence

horse   Date _____

hest

horse

horse
horse
horse
horse
horse

hest

Make a sentence

mouse   Date _____

mus   

mouse

mus

mouse (traced, 5 times)

Make a sentence

wolf   Date _____

ulv   

wolf

ulv

wolf
wolf
wolf
wolf
wolf

Make a sentence

panda   Date _____

panda

panda   panda

panda
panda
panda
panda
panda

Make a sentence

chicken   Date _____

kylling

chicken

chicken
chicken
chicken
chicken
chicken

kylling

Make a sentence

dinosaur   Date _____

dinosaur   

dinosaur   dinosaur

dinosaur
dinosaur
dinosaur
dinosaur
dinosaur

Make a sentence

elephant Date _____

elefant

elephant   elefant

elephant (traced, 5 times)

Make a sentence

cow   Date _____

ku   

cow

ku

cow
cow
cow
cow
cow

Make a sentence

butterfly Date _____

sommerfugl

butterfly sommerfugl

butterfly
butterfly
butterfly
butterfly
butterfly

Make a sentence

worm Date _____

mark

worm

mark

worm

worm

worm

worm

worm

Make a sentence

puppy Date _____

valp

puppy valp

puppy
puppy
puppy
puppy
puppy

Make a sentence

turtle Date _____

skilpadde

turtle

turtle
turtle
turtle
turtle
turtle

skilpadde

Make a sentence

turkey   Date _____

Tyrkia

turkey

Tyrkia

turkey
turkey
turkey
turkey
turkey

Make a sentence

hippopotamus   Date _____

flodhest

hippopotamus flodhest

hippopotamus
hippopotamus
hippopotamus
hippopotamus
hippopotamus

Make a sentence

tiger   Date _____

tiger

tiger tiger

Make a sentence

hen   Date _____

høne

hen

høne

Make a sentence

alligator   Date _____

alligator   

alligator alligator

alligator
alligator
alligator
alligator
alligator

Make a sentence

monkey Date _____

ape

monkey

ape

monkey

monkey

monkey

monkey

monkey

Make a sentence

spider Date _____

edderkopp

spider   edderkopp

spider
spider
spider
spider
spider

Make a sentence

shark   Date _____

hai

shark

shark
shark
shark
shark
shark

hai

Make a sentence

lion   Date _____

løve

lion   løve

Make a sentence

snail   Date _____

snegl

snail   snegl

snail
snail
snail
snail
snail

Make a sentence

kangaroo   Date _____

kenguru

kangaroo   kenguru

Make a sentence

fox   Date_____

rev   

fox

rev

Make a sentence

snake Date _____

slange

snake   slange

snake
snake
snake
snake
snake

Make a sentence

camel　　　　　　　Date _____

kamel　　　　

camel   kamel

camel
camel
camel
camel
camel

Make a sentence

octopus   Date_____

blekksprut

octopus   blekksprut

octopus
octopus
octopus
octopus
octopus

Make a sentence

rooster Date _____

hane

rooster   hane

rooster

rooster

rooster

rooster

rooster

Make a sentence

kitten					Date _____

kattunge

kitten

kitten
kitten
kitten
kitten
kitten

kattunge

Make a sentence

deer   **Date** _____

hjort   

deer   hjort

Make a sentence

ant   Date_____

maur   

ant

maur

ant

ant

ant

ant

ant

Make a sentence

dog   Date _____

hund   

dog   hund

Make a sentence

giraffe   Date _____

sjiraff

giraffe   sjiraff

giraffe
giraffe
giraffe
giraffe
giraffe

Make a sentence

cat   Date _____

katt

cat

katt

cat
cat
cat
cat
cat

Make a sentence

crab   Date _____

krabbe

crab   krabbe

crab
crab
crab
crab
crab

Make a sentence

zebra   Date _____

sebra   

zebra   sebra

Make a sentence

eagle   Date_____

Ørn   

eagle					Ørn

eagle
eagle
eagle
eagle
eagle

Make a sentence

rabbit   Date_____

kanin

rabbit

rabbit
rabbit
rabbit
rabbit
rabbit

kanin

Make a sentence

sheep   Date _____

sau

sheep

sau

Make a sentence

fish   Date_____

fisk

fish

fish
fish
fish
fish
fish

fisk

Make a sentence

bird Date _____

fugl

bird

fugl

Make a sentence

dolphin Date _____

delfin

dolphin

dolphin

dolphin

dolphin

dolphin

dolphin

delfin

Make a sentence

bee   Date_____

Bie

bee

Bie

bee
bee
bee
bee
bee

Make a sentence

hedgehog Date _____

pinnsvin

hedgehog   pinnsvin

hedgehog
hedgehog
hedgehog
hedgehog
hedgehog

Make a sentence

lobster   Date _____

hummer

lobster   hummer

Make a sentence

owl Date_____

ugle

owl

owl
owl
owl
owl
owl

ugle

Make a sentence

frog   Date _____

frosk   

frog

frosk

Make a sentence

pig   Date _____

gris   

pig

gris

Make a sentence

goat   Date _____

geit

goat

goat
goat
goat
goat
goat

geit

Make a sentence

dragonfly Date _____

dragonfly

dragonfly   dragonfly

dragonfly

dragonfly

dragonfly

dragonfly

dragonfly

Make a sentence

squirrel   Date _____

ekorn

squirrel   ekorn

squirrel
squirrel
squirrel
squirrel
squirrel

Make a sentence

parrot Date_____

papegøye

parrot   papegøye

parrot
parrot
parrot
parrot
parrot

Make a sentence

Made in the USA
Middletown, DE
27 September 2023

39550050R00060